SNAKES & REPTILES

A PORTRAIT OF THE ANIMAL WORLD

Andrew Cleave

TODTRI

This book was designed and produced by
Todtri Productions Limited
254 West 31st Street,
New York, NY 1001-2813
Fax: (212) 695-6984
E-mail: info@todtri.com

Printed and bound in Korea

ISBN 1-880908-26-3

visit us on the web!
www.todtri.com
Author: Andrew Cleave

Publisher: Robert M. Tod
Book Designer: Mark Weinberg
Photo Editor: Edward Douglas
Editors: Mary Forsell, Joanna Wissinger, Don Kennison
Production Co-ordinator: Heather Weigel
DTP Associates: Jackie Skroczky, Adam Yellin
Typesetting: Command-O, NYC

PHOTO CREDITS

Photographer/Page Number

James H. Carmichael, Jr 4, 8-9, 17 (top), 22, 23 (top), 28, 29 (top), 30 (bottom), 31, 32,
33 (bottom), 34 (top), 45 (top & bottom), 56-57, 61, 67, 69 (center), 77 (bottom)

Dembinsky Photo Associates
Barbara Gerlach 12, 19
Skip Moody 69 (bottom)
Stan Osolinski 34 (bottom)

Dwight Kuhn 62, 68

Joe McDonald 3, 6, 7 (bottom), 11 (top), 13, 20, 21, 23 (bottom) 27, 36, 37 (top & bottom),
38, 42, 46, 47, 53 (bottom), 55, 59, 63, 66 (bottom), 70 (top), 71 (top), 76

Nature Photographers Ltd
Colin Carver 18 (bottom)
Paul Sterry 78 (bottom)

Laura Riley 10

Len Rue Jr 39 (top)

Leonard Lee Rue III 43 (top), 79

Gail Shumway 14, 17 (bottom), 29 (bottom), 30 (top), 33 (top), 51, 52, 53 (top), 54, 58,
60 (top), 66 (top), 71 (bottom)

Tom Stack & Associates
Mike Bacon 39 (bottom)
David S. Barker 69 (top)
John Cancalosi 18 (top), 48-49
Christopher Crowley 77 (top)
David M. Dennis 7 (top), 16, 26
Jeff Foott 5
John Gerlach 70 (bottom)
Kerry T. Givens 35
Jack Stein Grove 11 (bottom)
Barbara von Hoffmann 15 (top)
Joe McDonald 15 (bottom), 44, 78 (top)
Mike Severn 49 (right)

The Wildlife Collection
Gary Bell 50 (top), 74
Ken Deitcher 60 (bottom)
Martin Harvey 24 (left), 24-25, 40-41, 64, 65, 72 (top left & bottom left), 75 (top)
Tim Laman 50 (bottom), 75 (bottom)
Dean Lee 72-73
Vivek R. Sinha 43 (bottom)

INTRODUCTION

The emerald tree boa inhabits forests of South America. The prehensile tail helps this arboreal species move with confidence and allows it to strike with at least half its body length at passing birds.

Reptiles have a poor reputation and few friends amongst humans. There are many misconceptions about their bodies and their way of life, many of them having originated in ancient times and persisting to the present day. The word 'reptile' actually means a creeping animal and is a reminder of the commonly held view of snakes in particular as being unpleasant creatures. Despite their unfortunate reputation, not all snakes are venomous, and most reptiles have a useful role to play in controlling insect or rodent pests.

Only in recent years has modern research been able to disprove the many misguided theories about the reptilian character.

As most reptiles are predators, they have a well-developed sensory system to help them find their prey and avoid danger. Their eyesight is good, and apart from snakes which have a different mechanism, they can focus their eyes by adjusting the shape of the lens. Nocturnal reptiles like geckoes see mainly in black and white, but most others have good colour vision.

Hearing is not an important sense in most reptiles and the internal structures of the ear are usually poorly developed. Most have no visible external structures, apart from a 'tympanum' or eardrum which is sensitive to vibrations transmitted through the air; these are then conducted along bones to the inner ear and the brain. Snakes have no external ear, and can only detect vibrations transmitted through the ground.

The aptly named helmeted iguana occurs from southern Mexico to northern Colombia. An agile and fast-moving species, it uses the skin on the nape in display and to deter predators.

Tortoises may appear docile and lethargic, but often this is far from the case. These two male tortoises in the American Southwest desert are engaged in a territorial dispute. This species is only active in the early morning, resting underground during the heat of the day.

THE REPTILE WORLD

Reptiles are described as being cold-blooded, but this is not very accurate. Their body temperature is largely controlled by their surroundings, but there are many things they can do to regulate this temperature and, if required, keep it at a higher level. Reptiles regularly bask in the sun, absorbing its heat through their skins when they need to raise their body temperature. They usually retreat to the shade when they start to overheat and wish to lower their temperature. Some species may be able to generate heat internally in their tissues and retain this to keep their core temperature up. The largest reptiles are able to maintain a more constant temperature than the smallest species, as their bulkier bodies contain more heat and have thicker skin and fatty layers.

Cold-bloodedness has some advantages over warm-bloodedness. Mammals must maintain their body temperature at a constant level, within very narrow limits. Even minor fluctuations are potentially serious. As a result, mammals constantly need food to provide the energy to produce the body heat. Reptiles, on the other hand, can cope quite well with a drop in body temperature; their range of temperature tolerance is far wider than those of birds or mammals. Very large reptiles do

This desert spiny lizard from New Mexico lives in an extremely arid environment and feeds mainly on other lizards. It seldom strays far from a secure bolt hole, such as a rocky outcrop or burrow.

Like other lizards, marine iguanas are cold-blooded and need to sunbathe each morning to warm their bodies. Some mature males develop the red colouration seen here.

A group of marine iguanas hauled out on a lava beach on the Galápagos Islands enjoy the equatorial sun. This is the only truly marine species of lizard, and these remote islands in the Pacific are the only place where they occur.

Green iguanas are widespread in Central and South America, but those from Costa Rica, shown here, are among the most attractively marked. This species spends much of its life in trees and is remarkably agile.

not require as much food to sustain them as mammals of the same body size, so they are able to inhabit regions which would be quite unsuitable for mammals. Deserts, for example, are ideal places for reptiles, as there is usually plenty of sunlight to warm them up and enough food to sustain them. Once they have had a meal, they can digest it at their leisure; some of the largest species can survive for several months between meals. A large mammal could not survive with such infrequent food. Consequently, the deserts are left to the reptiles.

Habitat and Body Temperature

A desert-dwelling lizard begins its day by creeping slowly from its nighttime hiding place in a burrow or under a stone. At this time, it is unable to make any rapid movements or capture food, but will just be able to manoeuvre its body into a position where it can be warmed by the sun. By lining up the maximum surface area of its body to face the sun, this animal can start to absorb radiant heat; it will also gain heat from the warm rocks it is basking on and the warm desert air. Blood vessels close to the skin then dilate to

A full-grown land iguana basks in the warmth of the morning sun. These large inhabitants of the Galápagos Islands can reach a length of 1 metre (3.3 feet), but are completely harmless to man.

Seaweed makes up the bulk of a marine iguana's diet. The head has to be turned to one side for efficient grazing, which is often performed below the water at high tide.

Since they venture into the water to feed, it is not surprising that marine iguanas are good swimmers, the tail providing most of the power for this exercise. These well-adapted creatures can remain submerged for surprisingly long periods.

absorb the heat and then distribute it around the body, warming the muscles and internal organs. These same blood vessels will later constrict and route blood away from the skin when the air temperature falls in order to conserve heat. Some lizards can flatten their bodies in order to increase the surface area available for heat absorption; some can even alter their colourings and become darker in order to gain still more heat.

Once a lizard's body temperature has been raised sufficiently to allow normal activity it will search for food, usually in the form of insects. Most lizards can move very quickly, and their excellent eyesight helps them spot fast-moving insect prey. In a desert the temperature may rise to very high levels by the afternoon. At this time, the lizard faces overheating. Retreating to the shade helps to reduce body heat and cut down on the absorption of more heat from the sun. If there is no shade the lizard may climb into a shrub and expose itself to cooling breezes in order to dissipate heat. It may be necessary to retreat underground in order to stay within the acceptable body temperature limits.

Once this is accomplished, the lizard can emerge into the open again, positioning itself so that minimum surface area is exposed to the sun and reheating takes place slowly. Changing back to a pale, more reflective colour also facilitates gradual heat absorption.

Another example of reptile ingenuity is found in the habits of marine iguanas of the Galápagos Islands. They spend their mornings like statues, lined up together facing the same direction to absorb sunlight. They rest on black volcanic rocks, which provide them with abundant heat, and when warm enough, plunge into the cold Pacific Ocean to feed on seaweeds. They can not tolerate this for long and soon emerge from the water to warm up once again, resuming their basking positions below the equatorial sun. There is great competition for the best basking sites, and the largest, dominant iguanas claim places where they can gain maximum exposure to the sun.

With all of these methods of thermoregulation available to them, reptiles can live in many regions of the world, apart from the very cold polar regions and high mountainous areas.

Eyesight

The only reptiles which seem to have a good sense of sight are the lizards, many of which hunt fast-moving prey like insects. Many lizards are colourful and perform attractive displays during courtship, making use of colourful parts of their bodies, such as throat patches. As a result, the ability to see in colour is essential. The agama lizards of Africa have brightly coloured heads and can often be seen standing on prominent rocks flicking their heads in a territorial display. Aquatic reptiles like crocodiles, alligators, and turtles rely more on their senses of hearing and smell to locate their prey, and also find their mates and warn them of approaching predators. They have serviceable eyesight and can spot movements close to them, but cannot form sharp images and are unable to focus for long on stationary objects. Most snakes have rather poor eyesight, usually only managing to detect moving objects which are fairly close to them. The freezing reaction of frogs when approached by a grass snake, for example, is a good defence mechanism, as the snake

will be unaware of its presence unless it makes a sudden movement. If it does move, the snake's lightning reflexes will make short work of a frog that gets too close. Only the tree snakes, which drape themselves along branches and catch birds and insects, have good binocular vision.

With its palette of orange-red and blue, the male agama lizard in breeding condition is among the most colourful of all reptiles. The bright colours help attract a mate.

A closeup view of an iguana from Mexico reveals the protective coating of scales so typical of reptile skin. Well-developed eyesight and sense of smell are also evident from the eyes and nostrils.

The throat dewlap (loose under-skin) of this Cuban anole lizard, photographed in Florida, is used as a visual signal to attract females and to warn off rival males. The dewlap is extended for a few seconds at a time.

Hearing and Vibration Detection

Snakes have a quite different sensory system from the lizards and other reptiles, which can hear. They seem to be unable to hear at all, thus making it impossible for them to hear the tune played by a snake charmer; instead, they are entranced by the pipe player's side-to-side movements. They also do not have external ears and eardrums, yet might be able to pick some very low-frequency vibrations by using the lung as a sense organ. Snakes mainly detect their prey or an approaching predator by sensing vibrations transmitted through the ground or whatever they are resting upon. As the whole of their body is usually in contact with the ground it can act as one large detector of vibrations. Anyone who has tried to creep up on a snake to take its photograph will know how difficult it is to achieve this without alerting the snake.

Some species of snakes, including the rattlesnakes and pit vipers, can detect prey by infrared radiation radiating from its body. They have sensory cells just below the eyes, which can pick up small changes in tempera-ture of only fractions of a degree and thus alert them to the position of a small mammal. These are highly sensitive structures and allow the snake to locate food in total darkness, if necessary. Some of the boa constrictors have sense organs along their lips which can also detect changes in temperature, but these are not as sensitive as those of the rattlesnakes and pit vipers.

Taste and Smell

The senses of taste and smell are important in snakes. The flickering forked tongue, still thought by some to be the snake's 'sting', is in fact picking up minute traces of airborne scents and transferring these to sensory pits inside the mouth, which then 'tastes' it. In the roof of the mouth is a special structure called Jacobson's organ, and this is linked to the brain by a branch of the olfactory nerve. The constant flicking in and out of the tongue is an efficient way of sampling the air for important chemicals. When the tongue is withdrawn into the mouth it rests neatly inside the Jacobson's organ, and the chemicals on it are detected by nerve endings.

In other reptiles, the sense of smell is of

The nonvenomous Everglades rat snake kills its prey by constriction. The snake can reach a length of 1.8 metres (6 feet) and, as its name suggests, it feeds primarily on rodents such as mice and rats.

The double-crested basilisk lizard is a highly active species from Central America. It can run at great speed both on land and over short stretches of water, a very useful skill for evading predators.

The Australian Outback is home to this shingle-backed, or stump-tailed, skink. When times are good and there is plenty of food available, the animal stores fat reserves in its tail.

The sand lizard is a characteristic species of heath-lands in western Europe and southern Britain. Hibernating during the winter, these lizards emerge in March to sunbathe in the spring sunshine.

great importance, and the part of the brain which deals with this is highly developed. The sense of taste is normally less powerful. As with snakes, the Jacobson's organ is used to detect airborne scents, aided by the tongue in some species which flicks in and out to collect scent particles.

Water Conservation

Many reptiles live in very dry habitats so conserving water in their bodies is extremely important. Lizards and snakes are best at conserving water, but it is not their scaly skins which help them achieve this. It is thought that snakes and lizards can lose almost as much moisture through their skin as birds and mammals.

While the high rate of mammalian respiration results in a great deal of evaporation from the surface of the lungs, the much slower breathing rate of reptiles causes only minimal water loss from the tissues. Many species of reptile have salt glands capable of removing salt from the blood and tissues—excreting it in crystal form dissolved in only the tiniest traces of water, thus reducing the need for the production of large volumes of liquid urine. Other unwanted salts in the blood are formed into uric acid, which can be removed with the minimum of water, unlike the waste material urea, which is produced by mammals and fish and has to be removed with large volumes of water. The marine iguanas of the Galápagos Islands can be observed nodding their heads and apparently spitting out salt. They are in fact ejecting it from glands near the eyes, and tiny white salt spots cover the surrounding rocks and other iguanas.

Lava lizards are found on most of the islands of the Galápagos. Their South American ancestors colonised these islands millennia ago, carried through the seas on floating vegetation.

19

Eggs

The reptilian egg contains everything required by the developing embryo. There is a food supply in the form of a rich yolk, water (contained in the albumen, or 'white'), and protective membranes in several layers, which prevent dangerous bacteria from entering but allow respiratory gases to pass through. The amnion is the layer which protects the embryo itself, and is a structure also present around the embryos of birds and mammals. The allantois is a larger membrane which acts as a 'lung' and an excretory organ, permitting the exchange of oxygen and waste materials. The chorion is a membrane which encloses the contents of the egg. In lizards and snakes the outer shell is leathery, but in turtles and crocodiles it is harder and calcareous, resembling the shell of a bird's egg.

The ability to produce these self-contained eggs has enabled the reptiles to colonise areas well away from water, unlike the amphibians, which must always return to water to breed.

These black rat snakes are just emerging from their eggs. The female will have laid between ten and thirty in a nest, perhaps sited in leaf humus in a hollow tree.

Three sensory methods of locating prey are located on the head of a diamond-backed rattlesnake. The eyes provide excellent vision during the day, while the tongue 'tastes' the environment. After dark, heat sensors located in pits between the nose and eyes come into their own.

SNAKES

The first snakes probably appeared on earth around 130 million years ago, according to the fossils found in rocks from the Cretaceous period. It seems likely that snakes evolved from lizards, losing their limbs as an adaptation to living underground. Most snakes now live aboveground, but they have not regained their limbs. Despite this, they are remarkably efficient creatures, being able to move with ease over a variety of terrains. Not only do they swim well, but also many species can climb trees. Additionally, they are able to capture fast-moving prey and can swallow animals whole which are much greater in diameter than they.

There are around 2,600 species of snakes known to science, and they are almost all carnivores, specialising in the capture of living prey. There are one or two exceptions, such as the remarkable egg-eating snakes, as well as the few species which will occasionally take dead food, but most species will only capture prey if it is actually moving.

Locomotion

Despite the lack of limbs, snakes move around very easily, being able to evade, capture, or pursue prey at great speed. Snakes swim without difficulty, curving their bodies

rather like eels. Some swim at the surface, whilst others are especially adapted to swim underwater and have flattened bodies to give them extra thrust. On land, snakes move by wriggling their body into a series of curves and pushing backward against stones and twigs. They can push themselves ahead quite quickly by this method, raising their head slightly for a better view of what is ahead. Snakes also use the concertina method for forward movement, drawing the body up into a series of horizontal folds and pushing forward. It then draws the remainder of the body up from behind the head and repeats the process. This method can be used for climbing trees as well,

To aid movement on a shifting substrate and to minimise contact with blisteringly hot sand, sidewinder rattlesnakes have perfected a movement that involves throwing the head and then the body sideways in an arc.

Although they spend much of their lives in water, anacondas are adept at climbing trees. Anacondas are the giants of the snake world, often reaching lengths in excess of 6 metres (19.8 feet) in parts of the Amazon where they are not persecuted.

A blood python from Indonesia emerges from a forest stream after cooling off. Most species of pythons are not averse to spending time in water and some will catch fish and frogs beneath the surface.

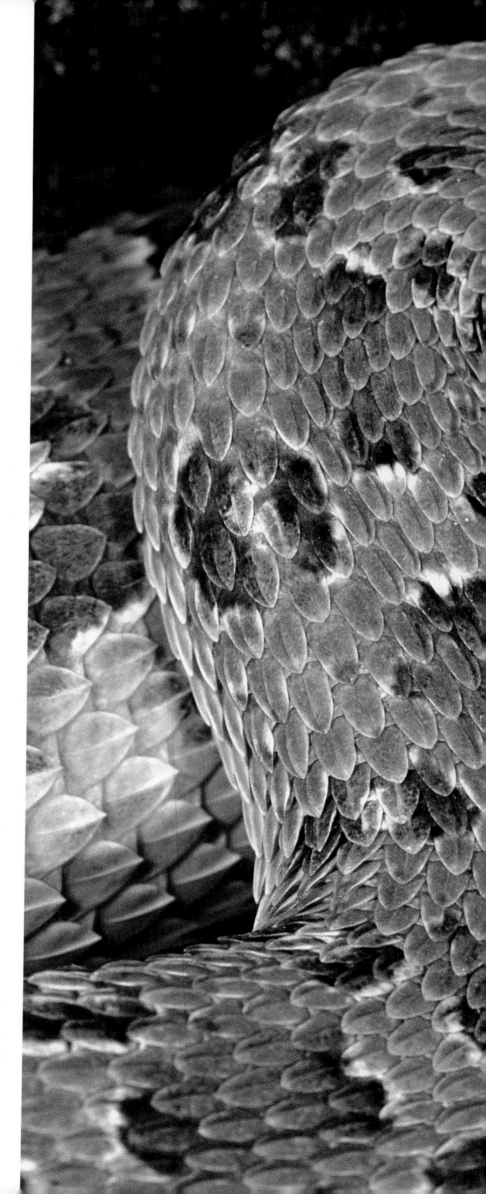

with the sides of the folds pressing against rough patches in the bark.

The so-called sidewinder snakes, which inhabit sandy deserts, move easily over loose and sometimes very hot sand by raising most of the body into a spiral and leaving only two points in contact at a time. Some of the largest and very heavy snakes like the boas, pythons, and anacondas use a method called 'rectilinear motion' to move forward. They are able to keep their body in a straight line and glide forward without any apparent muscular movements. What actually occurs is that scales on their undersides are being lifted up, moved forward slightly, and placed down again whilst others are drawn up behind them. This happens along the length of the body and is so well synchronised that the snake glides forward in a single smooth motion. This method can even be used to climb trees. Of all of the methods of movement, this is the least conspicuous and allows the snake to approach its prey unnoticed.

The Namagwa dwarf adder lives in desert regions in southern Africa. It can partly bury itself in the shifting sand, thus avoiding the direct sun and camouflaging itself from its small mammal prey.

The deadly horned viper of Africa uses camouflage to avoid detection. It can move in a sidewinder-type manner, the power in the sidestroke occasionally being sufficient to enable the snake to jump.

The Silent Hunters

For most snakes, the only weapons they have at their disposal are their jaws and teeth. Various methods are used to stalk and approach prey, and sometimes the snake lies in wait for the prey to approach it, but the attack always takes the form of a rapid lunge and a bite with the open mouth. It appears to take place at very high speed, but tests have shown that the final lunge of the head is actually slower than the speed of a human fist making a strike; it is the element of surprise that is important in overpowering the prey. The common grass snake of Europe is a typical species which feeds in this way. It is able to swallow its prey whole, usually a frog or small fish, whilst it is still alive and then retreat to a safe place to digest it. Because it is overtaken so quickly and is relatively small, the prey is unable to bite back or struggle very much and is soon overpowered.

Snakes which feed on larger prey must have

The patience of this long-nosed tree snake from southeast Asia has been rewarded. An unsuspecting lizard came within range of this camouflaged species, which captured it with lightning-strike quickness.

When all else fails, hognose snakes play dead, thus confusing potential attackers into leaving them alone. If turned over with a stick, the apparently dead snake will immediately turn on its back again.

The pine woods snake is a species most typically associated with damp woodlands. Here it feeds on frogs and insects, and usually hides among mosses and in rotting tree stumps by day.

some means of overpowering the victim before they can swallow it. They may themselves be at risk from flying feet and claws or the bite of a dangerous animal, so they must first kill the animal before it can be swallowed. Some snakes kill their prey by constricting it with coils of their body. They do not actually crush it, but they do suffocate it. After wrapping one or two coils around the body of their victim, they wait for it to breathe out and then tighten the grip a little

more. This makes it difficult for the victim to breathe in again, and eventually it dies of suffocation. All of the very large snakes kill their prey in this way. The boas, the pythons, and the biggest of all, the anaconda—which can grow to over 9 metres (29.7 feet) long—all capture and suffocate large mammals. Deer, pigs, and capybaras can all be overpowered and eventually swallowed, and there are instances of humans being eaten by giant anacondas in South America.

A Gulf hammock rat snake dines on a tree frog. Like other snakes, this species can dislocate its lower jaws in order to swallow prey too large for its normal gape.

This twig-mimicking snake from Madagascar demonstrates camouflage at its best in the animal kingdom. Insects and lizards stand little chance of spotting this predator as it lurks in the undergrowth.

This slender green vine snake is well camouflaged among the trailing plants in the Ecuadorian rain forest. It catches any unsuspecting insect or bird that strays within striking range.

The English name of this blunt-headed tree snake serves as a precise description of the animal as well. This species occurs from tropical Mexico through Central America to northern Bolivia.

The plains garter snake is widespread and common in the central states of North America. This species hibernates during the winter months, often congregating in large numbers at suitable sites.

Rainbow boas are widespread in the rain forests of Central and South America. They feed mainly on small mammals and birds, and usually hunt on the ground after dark.

There have been documented cases of reticulated pythons, shown here, growing to lengths of 7.5 metres (25 feet) or more. This huge snake comes from southeast Asia and feeds mainly on medium-sized mammals.

Constrictors

The constrictors all have teeth but do not have venomous fangs; despite this, they can still inflict painful bites when defending themselves. Once the prey has been killed the constrictor will loosen its grip by relaxing the coils of its body and spend some time examining its prey with its tongue. It eventually lines itself up with its mouth over the head of the prey and begins to swallow it. Because such snakes are unable to bite pieces off or chew prey, they must swallow them whole. This is a remarkable process to watch, as the snake must dislocate its jaws

The boa constrictor is among the most attractively marked of all snakes. As its name suggests, it kills its prey by entwining and constricting them, thus preventing breathing.

Rain forests of Central and northern South America are home to the venomous eyelash viper. This species uses its prehensile tail to secure itself among the branches, where it waits for passing tree frogs and lizards.

Although of great biological interest, the sight of an African rock python swallowing an impala is rather offputting. It does, however, clearly demonstrate the ability of snakes to contort their jaws in order to swallow large prey.

to allow its mouth to open wide enough to envelop the body of its prey. With teeth pointing backward to assist slipping the prey down in the right direction and repeated contractions of its body, the snake eventually consumes its food. The prey is always swallowed head first so that the limbs fold down more easily. The snakes which eat other snakes always start at the head as well, even though there are no limbs to get in the way, but it is possible that the scales would cause damage to the gut wall if they went down the wrong way. Snakes also produce extra supplies of saliva to lubricate the prey as it slips down the gullet and expand their elastic skin to accommodate the extra volume. Having accomplished this, the snake's body is hugely distended, and it slithers slowly away to begin digesting its meal. In the case of very large prey, this could take weeks, and the snake will remain largely inactive while its enzymes slowly break down the prey. Gradually, the large bulge diminishes, enabling the snake to feed again.

An anaconda gapes prior to swallowing its prey. This snake kills by constriction, and because of a disconcerting ability to dislocate its jaws, can swallow prey much larger than its head.

Venomous Species

The snakes which are unable to swallow their prey whole or crush it to death normally kill through poison. Even some of the small and apparently harmless species have a poisonous saliva, which they use to partially paralyse their prey. Some species have highly poisonous venom that they inject into the victim through two needlelike fangs, which can be folded away when not in use. The fangs are supplied with venom from large glands situated in the head, and these can pump out a deadly dose when it is needed. In most species the venom runs down grooves in the teeth and quickly enters the prey. In the case of the spitting cobra, the fangs point forward and the venom can be projected with deadly accuracy for a distance of 2 metres (6.6 feet). The venom is strong enough to cause permanent blindness if it enters the eyes of a mammal, including humans. This reaction probably has more to do with defence than prey annihilation.

The most venomous of all snakes is probably the king cobra, or hamadryad, which can grow to an impressive 5.5 metres (16.5 feet) in

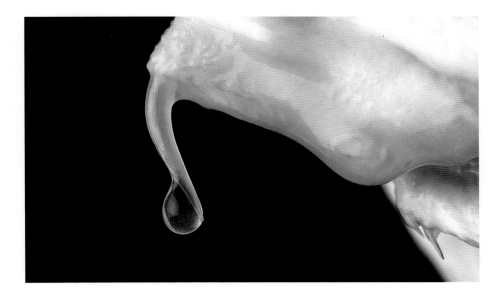

length. Its fangs are small and do not look very impressive, but they can deliver more venom than those of any other snake. The venom is strong enough to kill an elephant within four hours and can also kill humans. The king cobra is actually a rather placid species and only attacks under extreme provocation, so despite its powerful

The fang of a diamond-backed rattlesnake acts like a hypodermic syringe when the snake bites. A reservoir of venom at the base of the fang is compressed, forcing the deadly liquid into the body of the victim.

A diamond-backed rattlesnake in a defensive posture, poised and about to strike. If the rattle fails to deter the intruder, then the snake will unhesitatingly strike.

A northern copperhead displays its gape in a threat gesture. The two enlarged fangs are partly concealed by flaps of skin. This species is common in eastern United States and feeds mainly on small mammals.

As its name suggests, the mangrove snake of Thailand and the Malay Peninsula lives among forests and mangroves. It hunts at night for frogs and lizards, killing its prey with venom delivered by fangs in the back of its mouth.

venom is not responsible for as many deaths as the much smaller Indian cobra.

Members of the viper family have a very potent venom, delivered with great efficiency through their forward-pointing fangs, which lie in the roof of the mouth when at rest. The venom is slow to act, so after viperids, such as the rattlesnake, have attacked their victim and injected the venom they release their hold on the prey and let it move away. Depending on the

size of the animal, it can move off for some distance before finally succumbing to the poison. When it finally collapses, the viper tracks it down by scent or by the heat-detecting Jacobson's organ unique to the viperids.

The snake's teeth are not very strong and do not last for long, so there is a need for continual replacement. Many get broken during struggles with prey; these are replaced almost immediately by new teeth, which have been growing alongside them.

Sometimes referred to as water moccasins, cottonmouths are water-loving snakes that are highly venomous. The agitated individual in this photograph is gaping, revealing the cotton-white mouth from which its name is derived.

Sea snakes are among the most poisonous of all snakes. The venom of this olive sea snake, photographed on a coral reef in Australia, can kill its fish prey in seconds.

Following page: Because it is so difficult to spot, the deadly Gaboon viper is a much-feared snake in its African range, often lying motion-lessly on forest paths. When it strikes, the open mouth reveals large fangs.

Threatened with danger, this forest cobra has expanded its hood to make it appear even more menacing. Cobras are extremely venomous, and their bites kill hundreds of people each year.

The largest venomous snake in the world, the king cobra can reach a length of more than 5 metres (16.5 feet). Its diet mainly comprises other species of snakes, but this snake will not hesitate to attack man if provoked.

Eye markings on the back of the hood make an agitated cobra look even more intimidating to our eyes. When the snake is relaxed, it assumes a normal, elongated shape and both hood and eye markings disappear.

The puff adder is a highly venomous
snake species that is widespread in
Africa. It can flatten its body on
the forest floor and thus add to
its disguise among the fallen leaves.

The diminutive dusky pygmy rattlesnake
is a specialty of Florida and adjoining
southern states, most at home in the
dry grasslands of the Everglades. It feeds
mainly on small mammals and lizards.

Stunning colouration characterises
the temple viper of southeast Asia.
The open mouth shown in this
photograph reveals that the fangs
are partly concealed by flaps of skin.

The venom is actually a potent cocktail of various enzymes and proteins. It has a destructive effect on living tissue, although it does not have a part to play in prey digestion. The exact proportions vary from one species to another, but most venoms contain one element which attacks the nervous system and causes paralysis, another which paralyses the heart muscle and stops the blood circulating, a component which destroys body proteins, and one which either causes blood to clot or induces massive haemorrhages. In many species the dose varies according to the size of the prey; large quantities of venom are not wasted on small prey, but extra quantities are administered if the prey is large.

The rattle of a rattlesnake serves to announce its presence to animals that might otherwise be a threat. The rattle comprises several dry and horny segments at the end of the tail.

Named after the hornlike scaly projections on its nose, the rhinoceros viper of central Africa is a highly venomous rain-forest species. It hunts small mammals and birds.

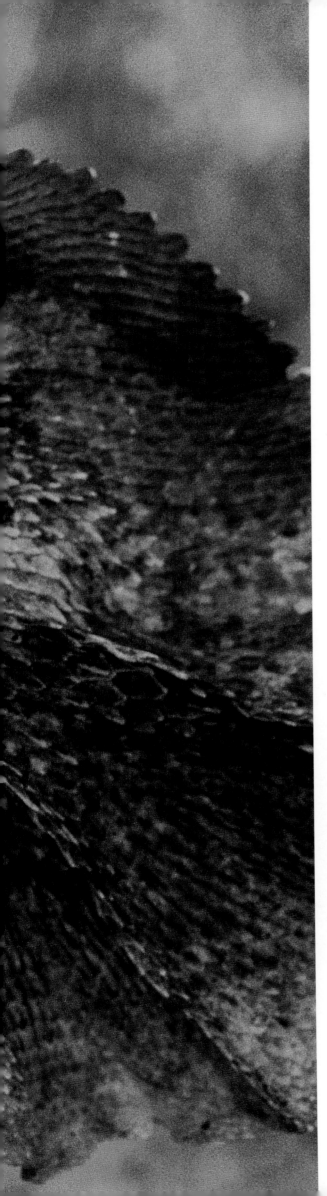

LIZARDS

There are about three thousand species of lizards, and they are the most diverse and widespread of all the reptiles. They vary in size from just a few centimetres to almost 3 metres (10 feet) long and exhibit many variations of shape, colouration, and feeding habits. Many are fast-moving ground dwellers which feed on insects, but there are some which have lost their legs and burrow underground, some which can glide through the air after launching themselves from the treetops, and still others which are slow-moving plant eaters.

Carrion Eaters and Poisonous Species

The most impressive of all the lizards is the Komodo dragon, which grows to a length of 3 metres (10 feet) and can weigh as much as 140 kilograms (308 pounds). It is a species of monitor lizard, found mainly on the island of Komodo and a few other Indonesian islands. It is the size of a crocodile, but lives on land and feeds mainly on carrion, which it finds

Like all monitor lizards, this species from Indonesia is a predator, most active during the day. The tongue is constantly flicked out to 'taste' the air for potential prey. Most monitors are not averse to feeding in water.

When threatened by danger, the frilled lizard spreads its coloured throat flaps—a bold and intimidating display.

49

A full-grown Komodo dragon can reach a length of 3 metres (10 feet), including the tail, and is large enough to tackle live prey, including wild pigs. Despite their size, Komodos are quick and agile.

Awesome in appearance, the Komodo dragon has been known to attack man. It is in fact a species of monitor lizard and is found only on the island of Komodo in southeast Asia.

getting near the large, dangerous adults.

Most lizards tackle their prey without the aid of venom, relying instead on speed, stealth, and strength, but there are two species which have poisonous bites. The Gila monster and the beaded lizard, both from the deserts of Arizona, have venom glands in their lower jaws. They are not linked with hollow fangs, as in the snakes. Instead, they simply release venom into the mouth with the saliva, which comes into contact with the prey when it is bitten. Their prey is usually nestling birds and newly born rodents, and they will also take eggs, none of which really requires venom to subdue them before they are eaten. In the long dry season, these two lizards live concealed in their burrows, hardly ever emerging, even during the cool of the night. They fast for several months, living off the food reserves stored in their fat tails. A captive Gila monster is said to have lived for three years without food. Once the rainy season comes around again and ground-nesting birds and rodents start to produce young, they emerge to feed and build up their reserves for the next period of fasting.

with the aid of its forked tongue and the Jacobson's organ. It is a large, powerful creature and is quite capable of killing deer, pigs, monkeys, or other large creatures with its claws and strong legs. It has teeth that help it tear chunks out of its prey and often gorges itself to such an extent that it has to rest in the same position for several days before it is able to move away. The young Komodo dragons behave more like conventional lizards, catching birds, rodents, other lizards, and insects, and they generally avoid

The colouration of this frilled leaf-tail gecko from Madagascar perfectly matches the tree bark on which it is resting. This camouflage enables the creature to avoid predators and to remain undetected by potential prey.

Geckoes

The geckoes are lizards with feet perfectly adapted for gripping smooth surfaces such as rock faces, tree bark, and the ceilings of houses. Their toes have ridged pads, enabling them to walk on ceilings and windows without any difficulty. Many homes in the Mediterranean countries and the Middle East have resident geckoes, and they are often encouraged as they keep rooms free of cockroaches and other troublesome pests. They hide during the day, emerging at night to feed, relying on their excellent eyesight to find food. The sense of scent does not seem to be so important in geckoes; their tongues are much thicker than those of other lizards and they do not flick them continuously. When a gecko spots prey, it moves carefully within range and then makes a lightning-fast dash, catching it with its mouth.

This Nicaraguan banded gecko displays the proportionately large head and eyes so characteristic of the group. Largely nocturnal, geckoes usually remain hidden during daylight hours.

Unlike most other lizards, geckoes do not have eyelids, the eyes protected instead by a transparent membrane. Rather ingeniously, geckoes clean this membrane with their long tongues.

Like its relatives, this Tokay gecko can climb surfaces that may appear smooth. The feet are equipped with a combination of claws and clinging toes, whose undersurfaces are ridged and covered in microscopic hairs. These produce a superb grip.

Few reptiles can rival the camouflage of this lined leaf-tail gecko from Madagascar. It not only resembles a twig in its colouration but also in its texture. The creature's ability to remain perfectly still completes the deception.

Unlike most other species of gecko, this Boehm's giant gecko is a diurnal species, relying on its excellent camouflage to keep it safe among foliage. A male is depicted here; females have duller colouration.

Following page: Jackson's chameleon is also known as the three-horned chameleon because of the armoured appearance of its head. It comes from Africa and spends much of its life moving slowly among the lush vegetation.

Chameleons

One of the most remarkable of all the lizards is the chameleon, famous for its ability to change colour and its amazingly fast and extra-long tongue. Several species of chameleons live in the Mediterranean regions, Africa, and Madagascar. It is a much slower creature than most of the other lizards, living in trees and relying on its excellent camouflage to remain hidden. It finds a good hunting position on a branch and then anchors itself firmly in place with its feet and tail. The tail is prehensile and can coil around the branch, and the feet have specially formed toes that can get a good grip on either side of the branch. Once it is fixed firmly in position, the chameleon waits for prey to come within range. Its eyes can move independently as they swivel around in search of suitable food. Should a fly alight nearby, a chameleon will turn its head in the insect's direction and then, quicker than the human eye can see, the tongue shoots out and back into the mouth, with the unfortunate insect trapped on the sticky end. Large prey, like a locust, might

The forward-facing horns on the head of this Jackson's chameleon are used in territorial disputes between males in the breeding season. Females' horns are much smaller.

Despite its showy appearance, this veiled chameleon from the Yemen is surprisingly well camouflaged when it moves lower in its bush. The colouration matches that of the lichens growing on nearby twigs.

The eyes of the Parson's chameleon, like those of other species, are capable of independent movement. In this way, the chameleon can be watching for food while scanning for danger.

Seen at close range, this male panther chameleon is a colourful and attractive animal. Like other lizards, its body is covered with hard scales, which protect it from attack and desiccation.

Chameleons are masters of disguise, able to adjust their body colour to match that of their surroundings. This panther chameleon from Madagascar demonstrates this ability to perfection.

be chewed once or twice, but usually the victim is gulped down and the chameleon is ready to hunt once again. The tongue may be longer than the chameleon's body when fully extended; an 18-centimetre- (7.2-inch) long chameleon can extend its tongue up to 30 centimetres (12 inches) from its body with deadly accuracy. When the tongue is not in use it lies neatly in the floor of the large mouth. The ability to change its colour to match its surroundings is a great help to the chameleon, as it can become almost invisible in thick vegetation; not only does this help it approach its prey, it also conceals it from the numerous predators which share the same habitat. The skin is covered with large numbers of pigment-bearing cells; the particles of pigment can migrate through these cells to produce variations in colour, and the reaction is usually very fast. Many chameleons have flattened, leaflike bodies to further aid camouflage, and some even sway from side to side to mimic leaves blowing in the wind.

A chameleon's tongue is its deadliest weapon. In many species it is longer than the body and for most of the time remains coiled inside the mouth. When the chameleon spots an insect, the tongue can shoot out in a fraction of a second, the sticky tip catching the prey.

The huge, prehensile-tailed skink from the Solomon Islands has developed the ability to grip branches and foliage with its tail. Other species have specially modified feet for gripping as they climb.

CROCODILES AND ALLIGATORS

The crocodiles and their relatives are the nearest living things we have to the extinct dinosaurs. There are about twenty-five species, including the alligator, caimans, and the gavial, ranging in size from about 1 metre (3.3 feet) long to over 7 metres (23 feet) long. They all inhabit the warmer parts of the world, usually preferring fresh water, although some live in estuaries and on the coast. They are all fierce predators, however, and some are very dangerous to humans.

Prey Stalkers

Like other reptiles, adult crocodilians spend much time basking in the sun, raising their body temperature, but they like to be near water and shade for quick cool-downs. Owing to their good sense of smell, they can detect carrion from great distances. If an easy meal, in the form of a large dead mammal, presents itself they will readily consume it, but they are also hunters and have developed many techniques for capturing live prey. Some will lie in wait in shallow water, with only the bulging eyes and the nostrils exposed, until a mammal comes down to the water to drink. They then approach cautiously and make a sudden lunge, seizing the animal by muzzle or foot and dragging it under the water. Crocodilians hold their prey below the water until it drowns and then drag it away to eat—on land or in the water. These reptiles' large jaws are armed with powerful teeth, which can tear pieces out of the prey, but they cannot chew it up, so instead must gulp down large pieces of flesh. They also use their feet to hold the prey down whilst tearing out large chunks of flesh; if the prey is in water, the crocodilians typically spin the body around to dislodge flesh. If the prey is too large to be consumed at one sitting, the crocodilians might stash it away. In the heat of Africa, for example, the flesh might start to rot, but this does not seem to bother most crocodilians. Indeed, it may be to their advantage to have slightly decayed flesh for easier digestion. These fierce predators have a bad reputation, but they are performing a very useful service, doing for the lakes and rivers what the vultures and hyenas do on land.

People sometimes fall victim to large crocodilians in boating accidents and other unfortunate circumstances, but usually this occurs when the crocodiles learn of a regular water-activity place, where they lie in wait for human prey in the same way they stalk animals who come to drink from the water. A number of the large species collect large stones and swallow them so as to make them-

selves less buoyant; this makes it far easier for them to sink back in the water with their prey and hold it under until it drowns. Small creatures are also regular prey; these are often snapped up with a sudden sideways movement of the head before the creature realises it is in any danger. Sometimes the crocodilians employ their powerful tail to flick creatures through the air toward their gaping mouths. Most crocodilians are very agile in the water, swimming with the aid of their flattened tail, their limbs folded back alongside the body.

If they encounter fish—a major part of the diet of many species—they catch them with a quick sideways movement of the jaws. These formidable reptiles bring the larger fish species to the surface and juggle them around until their heads point downward; thereafter,

Large fish are the Nile Crocodile's main dietary staple. The warm water in which these creatures are found produces an enormous amount of vegetative plankton upon which the fish feeds and so they grow large very quickly.

Getting a free ride, this turtle has hitched a lift on the back of an American alligator in Florida's Everglades. This creature might also be taking something of a risk, as the diet of young alligators sometimes includes the turtle.

Snakes do not always have it their own way. This water snake from Florida has been caught by a young alligator. No amount of struggling is likely to save it.

they swallow their victims head first. Crocodilians might also beat large, powerful fish against rocks or tree trunks to kill them first. The alligators of the Florida Everglades create pools in which to lie during the dry season, when the shallow waters recede. These alligator pools, excavated by powerful sweeps of the strong tail, are of great importance to many forms of wildlife. In the dry season they will be the only areas of deep water left and will contain large concentrations of fish, turtles, and birds. Areas lacking alligators—and, hence, the deep pools that they excavate—also are bereft of the rich wildlife that use them.

Parental Instincts

It was once assumed that the aggressive behaviour of the predatory crocodilians extended to their care for their young and that they would be more likely to eat them than protect them. This is now known to be far from the truth. Female alligators, for example, make nests of rotting vegetation in which to lay their eggs and they then guard these ferociously against all intruders. The nest is designed so that the temperature can be regulated by removing or replacing vegetation, and it usually floats to avoid the risk of flooding. When the young are about to hatch they start to squeak inside the eggs, and this is a signal to the female to remove some of the covering material to make it easier for them to emerge. The male might even help in this process in some species. The female then gently picks up the hatchlings in her mouth and takes them down to the water for their first swim. The young can find their own food from the outset, but they will stay in the vicinity of their mother for up to two years, benefiting from the protection she provides. She will even respond to distress calls made by the young and fiercely defend them from dangerous intruders.

A group of alligators resting in a favoured spot. Alligators are creatures of habit and when they find a good place to bask in the sun, they return day after day.

TURTLES, TORTOISES, AND TERRAPINS

Turtles, tortoises, and terrapins are all members of the order Chelonia, but they exhibit many variations and can be found on dry land, in forests, in fresh water, brackish marshes, on the seashore, and in the open sea. Turtles which spend most of their lives on dry land are usually known as tortoises. Terrapins are small turtles normally found in freshwater marshes.

The Shell

The most obvious feature of all the turtles is the shell—or, more correctly, the carapace on the upper surface and the plastron on the lower surface. These two protective structures, made up of about twenty to thirty bony plates, are fused with the ribs, the vertebrae of the spine, and the hip and shoulder girdles. They are covered with a horny material known as keratin, which peels away in dead specimens to reveal the bone beneath. The attractive colourings in the shells of many turtles lie in this keratin layer and not the bony shell beneath. In order to be able to grow, the shell is made up of separate plates, which can grow independently of each other. As the turtle grows, new rings of bony tissue are laid down around the edges of the shell plates, enabling the plates to retain their shape whilst increasing in size. The number of rings on each plate is a guide to the age of the turtle, although it is not quite as simple as counting growth rings in a tree stump. In some years, several rings might develop if there is good weather and plenty of food.

This parrot-beaked tortoise from South Africa is a particularly well-named species. Like its avian namesake, it uses reinforced bill plates to help cut vegetation and crack hard seeds and fruits.

Often spotted basking in the sun on a floating log, terrapins such as this ornate diamondback are ever alert to danger. At the slightest sign of trouble, they slip into the water and remain submerged for many minutes.

This closeup view of Blanding's turtle reveals how the head can be retracted into the safety of the shell when the animal is threatened with danger. This species feeds both on land and in water.

The English name of the box turtle perhaps derives from its high-vaulted shell. Despite its name, this species is primarily terrestrial, although it frequents wetlands during the summer months.

A Varied Family

The skull of a turtle has a flattened, box-like shape with two large eye sockets and a birdlike beak; there are no teeth, as in many other reptiles. Despite this they can eat a variety of foods, some of them being carnivores, others feeding on plant materials. Marine turtles and freshwater terrapins have short, strong limbs adapted for paddling and swimming, whilst the terrestrial tortoises have strong legs with claws for walking and scrambling. Both the tail and the head can be withdrawn into the shell if required, although some species are better at this than others. There is a great range of sizes amongst the turtles, with some of the largest marine turtles reaching lengths of over 3 metres (10 feet).

Courting and mating rituals of turtles usually involve a considerable amount of time. With these box turtles, the male has to cajole—and sometimes even bite and push—the female before the pair can copulate.

Widespread in North America, the painted turtle is common in muddy ponds and lakes. The young feed on aquatic insects, small fish, and amphibians while the adults prefer pond weeds.

Box turtles generally consume invertebrates. Following a recent downpour, a white-fronted box turtle from southern China dines on an earthworm.

This aptly named snake-necked turtle comes from New Guinea. It is exclusively aquatic and uses its long and flexible neck to catch small fish and tadpoles in the manner of a striking snake.

A female loggerhead turtle lays her clutch of soft-shelled eggs in a pit excavated in a sandy beach. Relatively few nests survive intact to the point of hatching—the eggs are a tempting meal for many predators, including man.

Mass-hatching is typical with most species of marine turtle. Here, several dozen loggerhead turtle hatchlings are scrambling out of the nest. They have an innate sense of direction when it comes to heading for the sea.

The Life Cycle

All of the turtles lay eggs, usually depositing them in nests dug out by the female in soft earth or sand. The large sea turtles might make migrations of hundreds of kilometres to favoured nesting beaches, where they make labourious progress up the sand to a safe zone above the high-tide line. Once there, and usually at night, they commence digging with their hind flippers until they have created a hole deep enough to accommodate around one hundred eggs. After laying them, the turtle eggs are covered over rather clumsily and then the turtle leaves, taking no further interest in them. Before

Although clumsy and vulnerable on land, all turtles must come ashore to lay their eggs. This normally occurs after dark, but this green turtle has been delayed until dawn, probably due to interruptions.

Largest of all the marine turtles, the leatherback slowly drags itself from the sea to lay eggs on a tropical beach. This turtle has a leathery skin covering its shell, not horny plates as in other species.

Hawksbill turtles range throughout the warmer oceans of the world. As with other species of marine turtles, the long limbs allow them to swim gracefully through the water in a seemingly effortless manner.

A loggerhead turtle swims serenely over the seabed. Like other reptiles, turtles breathe air and must return to the surface from time to time. They can, however, swim beneath the water for extended periods.

Although we may consider the gaping mouth of the alligator snapping up any creature to be a repellent sight, small fish find the wriggling, wormlike lure on the bottom of the mouth irresistible and are attracted to it— inevitably meeting their death.

they have had a chance to develop, many of the eggs will have been eaten by crabs, seabirds, feral pigs, dogs, or even humans.

Hatching is normally synchronised so that all the tiny turtles emerge at the same time, possibly reducing any individual's chance of being eaten. It is thought that the movements made by the first one or two hatching turtles act as the trigger for all the others to start moving inside the shells. Once out of their shell, they have to burrow through about 30 centimetres (12 inches) of sand to reach the surface and then head for the sea. The tiny turtles then have to run the gauntlet of ghost crabs and marauding seabirds as they make their first journey down the beach to the sea. Once they reach the sea the dangers are still not over, for sharks, hungry birds, and fish lie in wait for them. A few will survive, however, and they will spend many years wandering the

oceans before they return to complete the life cycle.

A visit to a turtle nesting beach in the daytime is fascinating: The trails made by the females are clearly visible in the sand; they look like the tracks left by large amphibious vehicles, yet lead to depressions in the sand high up on the beach. In such a situation, many turtles can be seen swimming languidly in the surf just offshore, and a number of these are certain to be males waiting for the opportunity to mate. Mating pairs can also be seen, the male clasping the female from above with his front flippers.

Most tortoises lay smaller numbers of eggs, but they also make nests and suffer the same problems of nest predation. The small tortoises of the Mediterranean region, for example, might only lay about six eggs, and these will be concealed in dry sand, where they take several months to hatch.

Tortoises are found in a wide variety of habitats, some of them surprisingly arid. This one, photographed in Kenya, uses its shell both as protection from predators and to reduce desiccation in the baking sun.

Lying among leaves on a riverbed, the matamata turtle uses camouflage to avoid detection by its prey. When a fish comes close enough, its neck shoots out and the hapless victim is devoured by the gaping mouth.

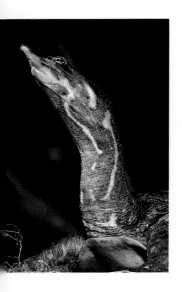

Soft-shelled turtles are a common sight in the Everglades and in other wetlands in the South. They bask on logs during the day and hunt for fish and other prey after dark.

Afterword

With very few exceptions, reptiles have always been exploited or badly treated by humans, and many species are now seriously endangered. The large sea turtles and giant land tortoises have long been exploited for food, and many isolated populations now face extinction. The giant tortoises of the Galápagos Islands in the Pacific once lived in colonies of thousands, but the whalers and seal hunters that visited the islands carried them away by the hundreds for fresh food on long voyages. The tortoises were stacked upside down, one on top of the other, in the ship's hold, where they would remain alive for up to a year. When the cook required fresh meat he would be able to slaughter one of the tortoises and make use of the flesh and the abundant oil it contained. The populations have never recovered from this overcollecting.

Many tortoises and turtles have been killed for their shells, which were used for making combs and ornaments. Crocodiles have long been used as a source of leather for making shoes, handbags, and belts. Oftentimes reptiles, particularly snakes, are killed simply out of fear; even harmless species like the European grass snake are sometimes killed on sight for no good reason, even though they are a useful species in keeping populations of destructive rodents in check.

The main threat to most reptiles now, however, is the destruction of their habitats by the spread of agriculture and tourism, the loss of forests, and the pollution of waterways. Although most countries have laws prohibiting the exploitation of endangered species, there is still a trade in skins and specimens for zoos and the pet trade.

Sadly, if this trend continues, it is likely that many more species will become extinct before the end of the century. Scientists are only just beginning to learn about the complex nature of the venom produced by many snakes, which may contain chemicals useful in pharmacy, and the eggs of many reptiles are useful in research on the development of embryos. It is likely that there are many more useful aspects of reptiles we know little about at present. Whether or not they are useful to us, however, the reptiles have been on this planet for millions of years living in harmony with their environment, and we do not have the right to bring about their sudden extinction.

Their numbers decimated by visiting sailors, Galápagos' giant tortoises are common only in a few highland areas. This group was photographed on the rim of Volcan Alcedo on the island of Isabela.

Giant tortoises once occurred on many of the islands in the Galápagos until hunting drove some races to extinction. Each race had a different shell appearance, the one photographed here being a so-called saddleback.

INDEX

Page numbers in **bold-face** type indicate photo captions.

adders, **24**, **45**
agama lizards, 15, **15**
alligators, **64**, **64**, **67**
American alligator, **64**, **66**, **67**
anaconda, 23, 24, 28
  constriction of prey by, **35**
anatomy of reptiles
  shells of turtles, tortoises, and
    terrapins, 69
  of turtles, 70
  of venomous snakes, 37
anole lizards, 15
aquatic reptiles
  loggerhead turtles, **75**
  marine iguanas, 7, **11**, 12, **12**
  sea snakes, 39
  senses of, 15

beaded lizard, 50
behaviour
  of hatching turtles, 76
  parental instincts of crocodiles, 67
black rat snakes, 20
Blanding's turtle, **69**
blood python, **23**
blunt-headed tree snake, **30**
boas, 3, 24, 28
boa constrictor, **33**
body temperature of reptiles, 7-10
  of crocodiles and alligators, 64
  habitat and, 10-12
Boehm's giant gecko, **55**
box turtle, **69-71**

carrion-eating lizards, 49-50
chameleons, 59-62
  Jackson's chameleon, **55**, **59**
  panther chameleon, **60**
  Parson's chameleon, **60**
  tongues of, **62**
  veiled chameleon, **59**
cobras, 37-38
  forest cobra, **43**
  king cobra, 37-38, **43**
  spitting cobra, 37
colour
  of chameleons, 59, 62
  changing, to control body
    temperature, 12
  reptiles' ability to see, 15
common grass snake, 27
constriction of prey, **17**, 28, **35**
constrictors, 33-35, **35**
cottonmouths (water moccasins), **39**
courtship
  colour used in, 15
  of turtles, 70
crocodiles, **64**
  hunting of, 78
  Nile crocodile, **65**
  parental instincts of, 67
  prey stalked by, 64-67
Cuban anole lizard, 15

desert spiny lizard, 7
diamond-backed rattlesnake, **20**, **37**
double-crested basilisk lizard, **17**
dusky pygmy rattlesnake, **45**

ears, 5, 16
eggs, **20**, 20
  of alligators, 67
  of loggerhead turtle, **72**
  of tortoises, 76
  of turtles, 72-76, **72**
emerald tree boa, **3**
environment
  in regulation of body temperature and,
    7, 10-12
  of reptiles, threatened destruction of,
    78
Everglades rat snake, **17**
evolution, of snakes, 23
eyelash viper, **34**
eyes
  of geckoes, **53**
  of Parson's chameleon, **60**
  of reptiles, 5
eyesight, 5, 15
  of lizards, 12

fangs, 37, **37**
  of temple vipers, **45**
  of vipers, 38
feeding
  by alligators, **64**

by carrion-eating and poisonous
    lizards, 49-50
  by chameleons, 59-62
  by constrictors, 33-35
  by crocodiles, 64-67
  by Everglades rat snake, **17**
  by geckoes, 53
  by lizards, 12
  in maintaining body temperature, 10
  by mangrove snake, **38**
  by marine iguanas, **11**, 12
  by Nile crocodile, **65**
  by rock python, **34**
  by snakes, 23, 27-28, **27-30**
  by turtles, 70
  by venomous snakes, 37-46
forest cobra, **43**
frilled leaf-tail gecko, **50**
frilled lizard, **49**

Gaboon viper, **39**
Galapagos Islands (Ecuador)
  giant tortoises of, 78, **78**
  land iguanas of, **10**, 12
  lava lizards of, **19**
  marine iguanas of, 7, **11**, 12, **12**, 19
geckoes, 5
  Boehm's giant gecko, **55**
  frilled leaf-tail gecko, **50**
  Nicaraguan banded gecko, **53**
  Tokay gecko, **53**
Gila monster, 50
green turtle, **72**
green vine snake, **30**
Gulf hammock rat snake, **29**

hamadryad (king cobra), 37-38, **43**
hawksbill turtle, **75**
hearing, 5, 16
helmeted iguana, 5
hognose snake, 27
horned viper, **24**
humans
  attacked by crocodiles, 65
  eaten by anacondas, 28
  geckoes kept as pets by, 53
  reptiles hunted by, 78
hunting
  of Galapagos Islands tortoises, 78
  by snakes, 27-28

iguanas
  green iguana, **9**
  helmeted iguana, 5
  land iguanas, **10**, 12
  marine iguanas, 7, **11**, 12, **12**, 19
  skin of, **15**

Jackson's chameleon, **55**, **59**
Jacobson's organ, 16, 19, 38, 50

king cobra (hamadryad), 37-38, **43**
Komodo dragon, 49-50, **50**

land iguanas, **10**, 12
lava lizards, **19**
leatherback turtle, **75**
lined leaf-tail gecko, **55**
lizards, 49
  agama lizards, 15, **15**
  anole lizards, 15
  beaded lizard, 50
  carrion eaters and poisonous species,
    49-50
  chameleons, 59-62, **60**
  Cuban anole lizard, 15
  desert spiny lizard, 7
  double-crested basilisk lizard, **17**
  frilled lizard, **49**
  geckoes, 53, **53**, **55**
  Gila monster, 50
  iguanas, 5, 7-12, 15, 19
  Komodo dragon, 49, 50, **50**
  lava lizards, **19**
  maintenance of body temperature by,
    10-12
  monitor lizards, 49, **50**
  sand lizard, **18**
  skinks, **18**, **62**
  snakes evolved from, 23
  water conservation by, 19
locomotion
  by horned vipers, **24**
  by sidewinder rattlesnakes, **23**
  by snakes, 23-24
loggerhead turtle, **72**, **75**
long-hosed tree snake, 27

mangrove snake, **38**
marine iguana, 7, **11**, 12, **12**, 19
matamata turtle, **77**
monitor lizards, 49-50, **49**, **50**
mouths, of constrictors, 33-35

Namagwa dwarf adder, **24**
nests
  of alligators, 67
  of turtles, 72
Nicaraguan banded gecko, **53**
Nile crocodile, **65**
northern copperhead, 37

ornate diamondback terrapin, **69**

painted turtle, **70**
panther chameleon, **60**
parental instincts of crocodiles, 67
parrot-beaked tortoise, **69**
Parson's chameleon, **60**
pine woods snake, **28**
plains garter snake, **30**
poisonous lizards, 49-50
prehensile-tailed skink, **62**
puff adder, **45**
pythons, 23, 24, 28
  reticulated python, **33**
  rock python, **34**

rainbow boa, **33**
rat snakes
  black, 20
  Everglades, **17**
  Gulf hammock, **29**
rattlesnakes, **45**
  diamond-backed, **20**, **37**
  dusky pygmy, **45**
  sidewinder, **23**, **24**
reproduction
  eggs for, **20**, 20
  of leatherback turtle, **75**
  parental instincts of crocodiles, 67
  of turtles, 72-76
reptiles
  body temperature of, 7-10
  eggs of, **20**, 20
  eyesight of, 15
  senses of, 5
  of turtles, 70
  water conservation by, 19
reticulated python, **33**
rhinoceros viper, **46**
rock python, **34**

sand lizards, 15, **18**
sea snakes, 39
senses
  of diamond-backed rattlesnake, 20
  eyesight, 15
  of geckoes, 53
  of hearing and vibration detection, 16
  of reptiles, 5
  taste and smell, 16-19
shells of turtles, tortoises, and terrapins,
  69, **78**
shingle-backed (stump-tailed) skink, **18**
sidewinder rattlesnakes, **23**, **24**
skin, of iguanas, **15**
skinks
  shingle-back (stump-tailed) skink, **18**
  prehensile-tailed skink, **62**
smell, 16-19
  crocodiles' sense of, 64
snake-necked turtle, **71**
snakes
  anaconda, 23
  black rat snake, 20
  blood python, **23**
  blunt-headed tree snake, **30**
  boa constrictor, **33**
  common grass snake, 27
  constrictors, 33-35
  cottonmouths, **39**
  diamond-backed rattlesnake, **20**, **37**
  dusky pygmy rattlesnake, **45**
  emerald tree boa, **3**
  Everglades rat snake, **17**
  eyelash viper, **34**
  evolution of, 23
  eyesight of, 15
  forest cobra, **43**
  Gaboon viper, **39**
  Gulf hammock ratsnake, **29**
  hognose snake, 27
  horned viper, **24**
  hunting by, 27-28, **27-30**

king cobra, 37-38, **43**
locomotion by, 23-24
long-nosed tree snake, 27
mangrove snake, **38**
Namagwa dwarf adder, **24**
northern copperhead, 37
pine woods snake, **28**
plains garter snake, **30**
puff adder, **45**
rainbow boa, **33**
reticulated python, **33**
rhinoceros viper, **46**
rock python, **34**
sea snakes, 39
senses of, 5
senses of hearing and vibration
  detection in, 16
senses of taste and smell in, 16-19
sidewinder rattlesnakes, **23**, **24**
temple viper, **45**
twig-mimicking snake, **29**
venomous, 37-46
vine snakes, 16, **30**
water conservation by, 19
water snakes, **66**
soft-shelled turtles, **78**
species
  of lizards, 49
  of snakes, 23
spitting cobra, 37

taste, 16-19
teeth
  of constrictors, 35
  of crocodiles, 64
  of Komodo dragon, 50
  of turtles, 70
  of vipers, 38
temperature, body, 7-10
  of crocodiles and alligators, 64
  habitat and, 10-12
temple viper, **45**
terrapins
  ornate diamondback terrapin, **69**
  shells of, 69
thermoregulation, 10-12
Tokay gecko, **53**
tongues
  of chameleons, 62, **62**
  of snakes, 16
tortoises, 5, **77**
  of Galapagos Islands, 78, **78**
  parrot-beaked, **69**
  reproduction of, 76
  shells of, 69
tree snakes, 15
turtles, **66**, 70
  Blanding's turtle, **69**
  box turtle, **69**, **70**, **71**
  green turtle, **72**
  hawksbill turtle, **75**
  hunting of, for shells, 78
  leatherback turtle, **75**
  life cycle of, 72-76
  loggerhead turtle, **72**, **75**
  matamata turtle, **77**
  painted turtle, **70**
  shells of, 69
  snake-necked turtle, **71**
  soft-shelled turtles, **78**
twig-mimicking snake, **29**

veiled chameleon, **59**
venomous lizards, 50
venomous snakes, 37-46, **37-39**
vibration detection, 16
vine snakes, 16, **30**
vipers, **24**, 38
  eyelash viper, **34**
  Gaboon viper, **39**
  rhinoceros viper, **45**
  temple viper, **45**

water conservation by reptiles, 19
water moccasins
  see cottonmouths
water snakes, **66**